# The Francophile's
# Quotation Book

French civilization is a civilization of
uniformity while the Anglo-Saxon one is
based on diversity.

*Edouard Balladur*
*French Prime Minister*

# The Francophile's Quotation Book

*A Literary Affair*

Edited by
JENNIFER TAYLOR

RÉPUBLIQUE FRANÇAISE

ROBERT HALE • LONDON

For Irene and David,
who can't keep away.

*Preface and selection © Jennifer Taylor 1995*
*First published in Great Britain 1995*

ISBN 0 7090 5311 8

Robert Hale Limited
Clerkenwell House
Clerkenwell Green
London EC1R 0HT

2 4 6 8 10 9 7 5 3 1

Printed and bound in Great Britain
by WBC Book Manufacturers Ltd.,
Bridgend, Mid Glamorgan.

# *Preface*

very year millions of Britons cross over to France in pursuit of the sun, a more relaxed pace, rural pleasures, and good food and wine at a reasonable price. This book is for all those discriminating millions.

There is of course a long tradition in this country of tabloid-style rubbishing of the French as garlic ridden frog-eating monkeys, vain, chauvinistic, and generally useless. Such ignorant prejudice has no place here. Fortunately, there is also a long tradition of francophile comment – in reports from travellers who liked what they saw – and enlightened appreciation of the many excellent aspects of French life. Reading through diaries and essays, or through the pages of Punch a century ago, the balance is pro French, with repeated criticism of the British for their atrocious lack of ability to speak the language, and for their insular outlook. But, it has to be admitted, the French are not perfect; chauvinism is a French word, OK.

I have French connections to declare: I had a French grandmother, and a French education. Years at the Lycée in London instilled into us from a tender age that France was mère des arts, des armes and des lois (in the poet Du Bellay's words). With what gusto we sang the Marseillaise on *prizegiving day, our thoughts on the long summer holidays stretching ahead. Learning history from the French viewpoint produced rather ambivalent feelings: definitely rooting for Joan of Arc, but a little uncertain about the defeat/victory of Waterloo.*

*I happened to be in Paris in 1990 the weekend the historic breakthrough took place in the Channel Tunnel, and there was jubilant press and television comment. But will the French really come over in hordes to stock up on sliced bread, tartan kilts and Burberry raincoats, and buy up cottages in Kent and the Cotswolds? Somehow it seems doubtful, although a degree of colonization seems to be afoot with French cafés sprouting up all over London.*

*There are many things which come to mind as quintessentially French: baguettes, runny Camembert, coq au vin, the smell of Gauloises, pissoirs, the TGV trains. My own list of favourite French things would include glimpses of jewel-like châteaux seen through the trees from country roads, films such as Les Enfants du Paradis and Jean de Florette, the novels of Raymond Queneau, fromage de chèvre beaten up with Armagnac . . . Any traveller to France will have his own.*

*And whether (like the Devil in James Joyce's story The Cat and the Devil) you can speak quite bad French very well, or even good French rather badly, whether you are heading for Mammouth in Boulogne to stock up on Le Creuset casseroles, or winding down with a kir in your dilapidated farmhouse in the Dordogne, whether your favourite Frenchman is René in 'Allo! 'Allo! or Gérard Depardieu, whether you are stuck in a jam on the Nationale 7 sometime in July or enjoying the après ski at Méribel, I hope you will find something in these pages to interest and amuse.*

JENNIFER TAYLOR

There is another shore, you know, upon the other side.
The further off from England the nearer is to France.

LEWIS CARROLL
*Alice's Adventures in Wonderland*, the Lobster
Quadrille

The French are a logical people, which is one reason the
English dislike them so intensely. The other is that they
own France, a country which we have always judged to
be much too good for them.

ROBERT MORLEY
*A Musing Morley*, 'France and the French'

Fair stood the wind for France
When we our sails advance,
Nor now to prove our chance
Longer will tarry.

MICHAEL DRAYTON
'Ballad of Agincourt'

We have only to read history from the days of Agincourt up to our later struggles with Napoleon I, to come to the conclusion that the two bravest and the most intelligent nations on the face of the earth have, from dynastic ambition, and a want of the people knowing each other, been ever engaged in inflicting mutual disasters, which have impeded for centuries the progress, civilisation, and prosperity of both.

CAPTAIN R.H. GRONOW
*Reminiscences and Recollections* 1810–1860

From London to Paris! – not very much further than from New York to Washington, yet this short distance divides two nations almost as different from each other as if a sea of fire rolled between them. Indeed, the narrow space of twenty-six miles of water, from Dover to Calais separates these long-hostile and still jealous powers – rivals alike in traditions, in history, in war, in commerce, in science, in diplomacy, in literature, and in language . . . .

To change from England to France is almost the transition from one planet to another.

JOHN W. FORNEY
*Letters from Europe*, 1867

Like country neighbours of uncongenial characters, we have never . . . continued long upon good terms, and have generally fallen out when any attempts have been made to . . . unite us more closely. Even when upon 'the most friendly footing', we have not heard with displeasure our neighbours abused, their peculiarities laughed at, and their weaknesses exaggerated.

SIR WILLIAM CLAYTON
*Journals* 1861–1914

I love France; and I am glad I saw it first when I was young. For if an Englishman has understood a Frenchman, he has understood the most foreign of foreigners. The nation that is nearest is now the furthest away. Italy and Spain, and rather especially Poland, are much more like England than that square stone fortress of equal citizens and Roman soldiers.

G.K. CHESTERTON
*Autobiography*, 1936

I have not always in my dealings with General de Gaulle found quotations from Trafalgar and Waterloo necessarily productive, and he has been very tactful about the Battle of Hastings.

HAROLD WILSON in 1967

Ask the travelled inhabitant of any nation, In what country on earth would you rather live? – certainly in my own, where are all my friends, my relations, and the earliest and sweetest affections and recollections of my life. Which would be your second choice? France.

> THOMAS JEFFERSON
> *Autobiography*, 1821

I am a citizen of the world; but if I were to adopt any country, it would be that in which I live at present (France), and from which I am determined never to depart, unless a war drive me to Switzerland or Italy.

> DAVID HUME
> in a letter to Gilbert Elliot, 22 September 1764

Every man has two countries, his own and France.

> BENJAMIN FRANKLIN

An Englishman who loved his Paris beyond any other city of the world once said to me, as we stood chatting in the Place de l' Opéra, 'If you find the central spot of this square, you may rap your stick upon it and say "This is the centre of the world." '

> LT.-COL. NATHANIEL NEWNHAM-DAVIS
> *The Gourmet's Guide to Europe*, 1903

France is the heart of the world.

> ARCHBISHOP MENDES DA CONCEICÃO SANTOS
> in a speech in 1920

The dial of Europe.

> LUDWIG BOERNE

Fraunce is a noble countre, and plentiful of wyne, bread, corne, fysh, flesh, & whyld foule. There a man shalbe honestly orderyd for his mony, and shal haue good chere and good lodging. Fraunce is a rych countre & a plesaunt.

> ANDREW BOORDE
> *A Dyetary of Helth*, 1542

France is the most beautiful kingdom after heaven.

> HUGO GROTIUS
> *De Jure belli ac pacis*
> an epistle dedicated to King Louis XIII, 1625

I am now upon the fair Continent of France, one of Nature's choicest Masterpieces; one of Ceres' chiefest Barns for Corn; one of Bacchus's prime Wine-Cellars, and of Neptune's best Salt-pits; a compleat self-sufficient Country, where there is rather a Superfluity than Defect of anything.

> JAMES HOWELL
> 'Letter to My Father, from Rouen'
> 7 September 1619; *Familiar Letters*, 1645

If I were God and had two sons, the eldest would have to be God after me, but I'd make the second King of France.

> attributed to MAXIMILIAN I, Holy Roman Emperor

What I gained by being in France was, learning to be better satisfied with my own country.

> DR SAMUEL JOHNSON
> James Boswell's *Life of Johnson*

All my life I have thought of France in a certain way. This is inspired by sentiment as much as by reason. The emotional side of me tends to imagine France . . . as dedicated to an exalted and exceptional destiny. Instinctively I have the feeling that Providence has created her either for complete successes or for exemplary misfortunes. If, in spite of this, mediocrity shows in her acts and deeds, it strikes me as an absurd anomaly, to be imputed to the faults of Frenchmen, not to the genius of the land . . . France cannot be France without greatness.

> PETER ABELARD in the 12th century

Kings, aristocrats, and tyrants, whoever they may be, are slaves in rebellion against the sovereign of the earth, which is mankind, and against the legislator of the universe, which is nature.

> FRANÇOIS-MARIE DE ROBESPIERRE
> *Déclaration des droits de l'homme*, 24 April 1793

Daily experience shows that the French are instinctively drawn by power; they do not love liberty – equality alone is their idol. Now equality and tyranny are secretly connected.

> FRANÇOIS-RENÉ DE CHATEAUBRIAND
> *Mémoires d'outre-tombe*

Without the Consulate and the Empire, the revolution would have been only a grand drama, leaving grand revolutions but no traces: the revolution would have been drowned in the counter-revolution. The contrary, however, was the case. Napoleon rooted the revolution in France, and introduced throughout Europe, the principal benefits of the crisis of 1789 . . . He purified the revolution in separating the truths which it contained from the

passions that, during its delirium, disfigured it. He en-
nobled the people in giving them the consciousness of
their force . . . The Emperor may be considered as the
Messiah of the new ideas.

    W.M. THACKERAY
    *The Paris Sketch Book*, 1840

*First Citoyen:* 'Was it not a fine change to cry *"Vive l'Empereur"*
for a whole week instead of *"Vive la République"*?'
*Second Citoyen:* 'Ah mon brave, it was magnificent!'
From *Punch* in 1896

Bonaparte is not great because of his words, speeches or writings . . . but because he created a strong and powerful government, a code of laws which has been adopted in several countries, courts of law, schools and a solid, active, intelligent administration with which we are still living.

> FRANÇOIS-RENÉ DE CHATEAUBRIAND
> *Mémoires d'outre-tombe*

The simple thing is to consider the French as an erratic and brilliant people, dressed either in blue blouses and berets or trick suits and Charvet ties, who have all the gifts except that of running their country.

> JAMES CAMERON
> writing in the *News Chronicle*, January 1954

A fickle nation

> NAPOLEON BONAPARTE

The fickleness of the French exemplified indeed! Louis Napoleon is proclaimed Emperor and this by a people who but twelve months ago elected him President simply because he vowed to keep unchanged the name and statutes of a Republic and now they see this man breaking his oath and forming a style of government far more arbitrary than that of Louis Philippe whom they deposed because they thought his laws illiberal.

> MARIE LOUISE DE LA RAMÉE (OUIDA)
> *Journal*, 1852, written when she was thirteen

A conservative nation which likes even its disorders to have a cachet of organized continuity.

> ARTHUR KOESTLER

France prides itself on being very old, on being not only the first-born among modern nations but the heir of the ancient world, the transmitter to the West of Mediterranean civilization.
>HELEN HILL MILLER
'The Spirit of Modern France', 1934

All my life I have been grateful for the contribution France has made to the glory and culture of Europe – above all for the sense of personal liberty and the rights of man that has radiated from the soul of France.
>SIR WINSTON CHURCHILL
in a speech in Parliament, 2 August 1944

France is the working model of Europe; like a clock with the clockwork showing clearly in a glass-case. There the movements occur rapidly, sharply, and logically, which appear elsewhere more slowly, more confusedly.
>G.K. CHESTERTON
*Generally Speaking*, 1928

Old France, weighed down with history, prostrated by wars and revolutions, forever vacillating between greatness and decline, but revived, century after century, by the genius of renewal.
>CHARLES DE GAULLE
*War Memoirs*

Patriotism takes the place of religion in France. In the service of *la patrie* the doing of one's duty is elevated into the sphere of exalted emotion.
>WILLIAM C. BROWNELL
*French Traits*, 1889

France is divided into 43 million Frenchmen.
> PIERRE DANINOS
> *Les Carnets du Major Thompson*, 1954

If the French were to play cricket they would all want to be 'batsmen' – the cynosure of all eyes – at the same time, just as nearly all of them want to be Prime Minister.
> JEAN FAYARD

The French have vanity, levity, independence, and caprice, with an unconquerable passion for glory. They will as soon do without bread as without glory.
> NAPOLEON BONAPARTE

How can you be expected to govern a country that has two hundred and forty-six kinds of cheese?
> CHARLES DE GAULLE

A country where the impossible always happens and the inevitable never does.
> ANON

The French have very magnificent ideas, and it is their delight to be laying magnificent plans. They begin works with a degree of vigour and expense that exhausts both their patience and their finances.
> THOMAS BENTLEY
> *Journal of a Visit to Paris*, 1776

There is nothing better than what the French do well, and nothing worse than what they do badly.
> POPE BENEDICT XIV

The French are the only people, except the Greeks, who have been at once philosophers, poets, orators, historians, painters, architects, sculptors and musicians . . . And, in common life, they have, in great measure, perfected that art, the most useful and agreeable of any, *l'Art de Vivre*, the art of society and conversation.

> DAVID HUME
> *Essays Moral and Political*, 1741

A Frenchman must be always talking, whether he knows any thing of the matter or not; an Englishman is content to say nothing, when he has nothing to say.

> DR SAMUEL JOHNSON
> James Boswell's *Life of Johnson*

A Frenchman not only means nothing beyond common civility, by the plentiful shower of compliments which he pours on every stranger; but also, he takes it for granted, that the stranger knows that nothing more is meant.

> JOHN MOORE
> *A View of Society and Manners, in France, Switzerland, Germany*, 1779

The hospitality of manners in France is not comple-mented by real hospitality of thought.

> HENRI FRÉDÉRIC AMIEL
> *The Private Journal of Henri Frédéric Amiel*

Everything is on such a clear financial basis in France . . . No one makes things complicated by becoming your friend for any obscure reason.

> ERNEST HEMINGWAY
> *The Sun Also Rises*

Nearly half a century of experience amongst them has taught me that there is much to learn and much that is worthy of imitation in France . . . They are less prejudiced than we islanders, and are much more citizens of the world than ourselves. I have received an immense amount of courtesy in France; and if there be less of solid friendship – which, however, in England is based too often on a similarity of birth, position, and wealth – in France, you have, at least, a greater chance than in England of making a friend of a man who neither looks to your ancestors nor your amount of riches before he proffers you the most sincere intimacy, and, if necessary, disinterested aid, purely on the ground of your own merit and character.

CAPTAIN R.H. GRONOW
*Reminiscences and Recollections* 1810–1860

I liked much what little I saw of the French people. They are accused of vanity; and doubtless they have it, and after a more obvious fashion than other nations; but their vanity, at least, includes the wish to please; other people are necessary to them; they are not wrapped up in themselves; not sulky . . . There is a good deal of touchiness, I suspect, among them – a good deal of ready-made heat, prepared to fire up in case the little commerce of flattery and sweetness is not properly carried on. But this is better than ill-temper.

LEIGH HUNT
*Autobiography*

The French complain of everything, and always.
NAPOLEON BONAPARTE

In France, all is clockwork, all is order. They make no mistakes. Every third man wears a uniform, and whether he be a marshal of the empire or a brakeman, he is ready and perfectly willing to answer all your questions with tireless politeness.

> MARK TWAIN
> *The Innocents Abroad*

*Messieurs les Anglais, tirez les premiers.*

> attributed to the COMTE D'AUTEROCHE
> at the French victory of Fontenoy in 1745

*Editor's note*: This is the legend learnt by every *lycéen* – that the chivalrous Count invited the British to be kind enough to be first to fire. But reference books suggest that it may be apocryphal, while Pierre Daninos, in his book *Les Carnets du Major Thompson*, has an alternative version: that the Count, seeing the British suddenly loom out of the fog, called out to his own men, '*Messieurs! les Anglais! Tirez les premiers!*'

Their beggars are the very politest beggars I ever knew; in other places a traveller is addressed with a piteous whine, or a sturdy solemnity, but a French beggar shall ask your charity with a very genteel bow, and thank you for it with a smile and a shrug.

> OLIVER GOLDSMITH
> *The Citizen of the World*

French honesty arises not perhaps from the love of justice, but from a repugnance to violence or force. They are a complaisant people, and would not rob you without first asking your consent, and making you an accomplice in your own wrong.

> WILLIAM HAZLITT
> *Travelling Abroad*

'I implore your pardon for having deranged you, *Monsieur le Gendarme*, but might I dare ask you to have the goodness to do me the honour to indicate to me the way to the Street of the Cross of the Little-Fields?'

From *Punch* in 1877

Their civility to strangers is not half so great as their admiration of themselves. Every thing that belongs to them and their nation is great; magnificent beyond expression; quite romantic! every garden is a paradise, every hovel a palace, and every woman an angel.

OLIVER GOLDSMITH
*The Citizen of the World*

The passion of nearly every Frenchman is to pass for a wit.

MONTESQUIEU
*Lettres persanes*

'Witty' is a wretched translation of *spirituel*. To be *spirituel* is to be witty in a spiritual way. It involves the active interposition of mind, and what is known as the light touch.

WILLIAM C. BROWNELL
*French Traits*, 1889

The majority of the French people are blind, credulous, ignorant, ungrateful, malicious and stupid. In a word they are mostly bourgeois.

GEORGE SAND
making a political point in a letter to
Mazzini, 30 September 1848

It was disappointing that French wit did not on these occasions elaborate any jest more sparkling than 'Ah! Les Anglaises!' though the inhabitants seemed to find the humour of the situation satiatingly expressed in this simple formula.

E. SOMERVILLE & MARTIN ROSS
*In the Vine Country*

France was long a despotism tempered by epigrams.
> THOMAS CARLYLE
> *The French Revolution*

Whenever I hear French spoken as I approve, I find myself quietly falling in love.
> E.R. BULWER-LYTTON
> *Lucile*

The most perspicuous and pointed language in the world.
> SAMUEL TAYLOR COLERIDGE

A language . . . badly fitted for music
> WOLFGANG AMADEUS MOZART

What is not clear is not French.
> RIVAROL
> *Discours sur l'Universalité de la langue*
> *française*, 1784

To be introduced to the People of high quality, it is absolutely necessary to be master of the Language, for it is not to be imagined that they will take pains to understand anybody, or to correct a stranger's blunders.
> THOMAS GRAY
> in a letter to Thomas Ashton from Paris,
> 21 April 1739

French people hate broken French worse than most of us hate broken English.
> FRANK MOORE COLBY
> 'Profession of a Gallows Maniac',
> *The Margin of Hesitation*

In Paris they simply stared when I spoke to them in
French; I never did succeed in making those idiots understand their own language.
    MARK TWAIN

No matter how politely and distinctly you ask a Parisian a
question, he will persist in answering you in French.
    FRAN LEBOWITZ
    *Metropolitan Life*, 1978

The girls (in common with the people in this part of
France) spoke the language so barbarously that I could
not understand what they said. They were highly amused
with my bad French.
    WASHINGTON IRVING in Toulouse
    *Notes and Journal of Travel in Europe*, 22 August
    1804

Later, I was 'invited' to study French. 'You'll never be
able to talk it, but if I were you, I'd try to read it' was his
word. I append here the method of instruction. Give an
English boy the first half of *Twenty Thousand Leagues
under the Sea* in his native tongue. When he is properly
intoxicated, withdraw it and present to him the second
half in the original . . .
    The official study of the French language in the
English schools of those days assumed that its literature
was 'immoral'; whereas the proper slant of accents and
the correct assignment of genders was virtuous. In my
own interests, then, I made my 'graves' and 'acutes' as
nearly vertical as might be, while my calligraphy served
as a fig-leaf to cover those delicate problems of sex in
inanimate objects.
    RUDYARD KIPLING
    *Souvenirs of France*

Never go to France
Unless you know the lingo,
If you do, like me,
You will repent, by jingo.
THOMAS HOOD
'French and English'


*Tant pis* and *tant mieux* being two of the great hinges in
French conversation, a stranger would do well to set him-
self right in the use of them, before he gets to Paris.
LAURENCE STERNE
*A Sentimental Journey*


For all one's stock, one need but draw
On some half-dozen words like these –
*Comme ça – par là – là bas – ah ha!*
They'll take you all through France with ease.
THOMAS MOORE
*The Fudge Family in Paris*, 1818


In France we contented ourselves with devising a pro-
nounceable variation of the existing name. If a road was
called *La Rue du Bois*, we simply called it 'Roodiboys'.
*Etaples* was modified to 'Eatables' and *Sailly-la-Bourse*
became 'Sally Booze'.
IAN HAY in France during the First World War,
*Carrying On*


Into the face of the young man who sat on the terrace of
the Hotel Magnifique at Cannes there had crept a look of
furtive shame, the shifty, hangdog look which announces
that an Englishman is about to talk French.
P.G. WODEHOUSE
*The Luck of the Bodkins*

*Le Sportsman Français*
(as seen by *Punch* in 1896)

Si vous êtes un fluent English speaker, et si vous avez un 'O' Level français, Franglais est un morceau de gâteau.
MILES KINGTON
*Let's Parler Franglais*, 1979

*Le sportsman, le challenge, le weekend, le fair play, le football, le jogging, le T-shirt*
*le briefing, le brainstorming, le headbanging*
*le fast-food, le hamburger*
*le Shuttle, le checklist, le cash'n'carry, surbooker.*
some words (which Minister of Culture Jacques Toubon failed to make illegal in May 1994) to help get by in France

You will not be able to shower your fiancée with bouquets or meet her at a secret rendezvous. Or buy her haute couture clothes. There will be great difficulties having a ménage-à-trois. Crime passionnel is out of the question . . .
ANTHONY STEEN MP
in his retaliatory French Words (Prohibition) Bill, seeking restrictions on the use of French words in English, July 1994
*Editor's note*: MPs rejected this Bill in Parliament by a majority of 100. But the French press took it seriously.

It is good to be on your guard against an Englishman who speaks French perfectly; he is very likely to be a cardsharper or an attaché in the diplomatic service.
W. SOMERSET MAUGHAM

They are a loyal, a gallant, a generous, an ingenious, and good-temper'd people as is under heaven – if they have a fault, they are too *serious*.
LAURENCE STERNE
*A Sentimental Journey*

The French are frivolous in their amusements, but serious and sober in their tastes.
LOUIS DE BONALD
*Maximes et Pensées*

One cannot play with the nerves of the French people.
JACQUES DELORS
announcing that he would not run for the French presidency, December 1994

A Frenchman who, with a fund of virtue, learning and good sense, has the manners and good breeding of his country, is the perfection of human nature.
LORD CHESTERFIELD
in a letter, 6 March 1747

The Almighty in His infinite wisdom did not see fit to create Frenchmen in the image of Englishmen.
SIR WINSTON CHURCHILL
in a speech in Parliament, 10 December 1942

Frenchmen have an unlimited capacity for gallantry and indulge it on every occasion.
MOLIÈRE
*Le Sicilien ou l'Amour peintre*

Every Frenchman takes an intelligent interest in the affairs of his country.

From *Punch* in 1877

They have certainly got the credit for understanding more of love, and making it better than any other nation upon earth; but for my own part, I think them errant bunglers, and in truth the worst set of marksmen that ever tried Cupid's patience. To think of making love by *sentiments!*

LAURENCE STERNE
*A Sentimental Journey*

It's true that the French have a certain obsession with sex, but it's a particularly adult obsession. France is the thriftiest of all nations; to a Frenchman sex provides the most economical way to have fun.

ANITA LOOS
*Kiss Hollywood Good-bye*

One becomes aware in France, after having lived in America, that sex pervades the air. It's there all around you, like a fluid.

HENRY MILLER
in an interview

Nobody who has not lived intimately in and with Paris can appreciate the unique savour of that word *femmes*.

ARNOLD BENNETT
*Paris Nights*, 1913

In France, any pretty woman is queen.

C.-S. FAVART
*Les Trois Sultanes*

The truth is that coquetry, which is a defect in our eyes, is a quality of the Frenchwoman. It is a virtue which consecrates as it were the possession of natural attractions. In France always *le charme prime la beauté*, and coquetry there is the science of charm in women.

In elegance, in intelligence, in self-possession, in poise, it would be difficult to find exceptions in other countries to rival the average Parisienne.

> WILLIAM C. BROWNELL
> *French Traits*, 1889

French woman dips into love like a duck into water, tis but a shake of the feathers & wag of the tail & all is well again but an Englishwoman is like a heedless swan venturing into a pool who gets drowned.

> WASHINGTON IRVING
> *Journal*, 1822

. . . Frenchwomen and their impudent confidence in the power of sex.

> KATHERINE MANSFIELD
> *Journal*

The women of France interfere in the politics of the Country, and often give a decided Turn to the Fate of Empires.

> ANNE WILLING BINGHAM
> in a letter to Thomas Jefferson, *c.* 1783–86

In France a woman will not go to sleep until she has talked over affairs of state with her lover or her husband.

> attributed to CARDINAL MAZARIN, *c.* 1650

France is the only place where you can make love in the afternoon without people hammering on your door.

> BARBARA CARTLAND
> quoted in the *Guardian*, December 1984

It is unthinkable for a Frenchman to arrive at middle age without having syphilis and the *Croix de la Légion d'honneur*.

    attributed to ANDRÉ GIDE

A country where it is often useful to exhibit one's vices, and invariably dangerous to exhibit one's virtues.

    NICOLAS CHAMFORT

Private life is exactly that and it is the same for everyone . . . It just does not interest me if Balladur pays visits to Madame Claude. I just want him to be a good prime minister.

    GILLES DREYFUS
    Paris lawyer to the famous, quoted
    in the *Sunday Times*, November 1993

Amusing that the typical figure of that country in so many people's imagination is a saucy girl with little or nothing on, whereas in reality it is an old woman in mourning.

    E.V. LUCAS
    *365 Days and One More*

There is, in fact, no branch of human activity in which one is not liable, in France, to find a woman engaged. Women, indeed, are not priests; but priests are, more or less, women. They are not in the army, it may be said; but then they *are* the army. They are very formidable. In France one must count with the women.

    HENRY JAMES
    *A Little Tour in France*, 1884

I hold the Parisian Old Woman to be the most remarkable individual of her sex and age to be found in the
whole world.
> GEORGE AUGUSTUS SALA
> *Paris Herself Again in 1878–9*

In every building of Paris there is a concierge, to serve as
a human watchdog. Whoever you are, she knows about
you.
> TED MILLS and STEVEN WHITE
> 'Maurice Chevalier's Paris', NBC TV, 1957

The French are a 'stuffy' nation; but they *do* hang their
bedding out of the windows in the morning to air. This
is more than can be said of the English.
> ARNOLD BENNETT
> *Journals*, 16 March 1905

Honour the French! They have taken good care of the
two greatest needs – good eating and civic equality.
> HEINRICH HEINE

*Liberté! Fraternité! Sexualité!*
> graffito in the Paris Métro, 1980s

Morality and decency they know nothing of, but yet with
benefit we might exchange a little of our morality for
some of their cooking virtues.
> DOROTHY NEVILL
> *Letter to a Friend*, 1871

A blaspheming Frenchman is a spectacle more pleasing
to the Lord than a praying Englishman.
> HEINRICH HEINE

The French are better *consumers* than we are. They will buy nothing which is not what they want, will buy no more than they want, and will take care that what they buy is fitted and finished in the precise manner which suits them best. The consequence is, that France, as a country, has a kind of finish which England lacks.

 WALTER BAGEHOT
 'One Difference Between England and France',
 *The Economist*, 12 September 1868


When marketing one should never be content with the goods displayed on the stalls. The more difficult Madame is, the more she will be respected.

 WINIFRED LADY FORTESCUE
 *Perfume from Provence*


Everything French suits exactly every Frenchman.

 WILLIAM C. BROWNELL
 *French Traits*, 1889


The French trades people display a very pretty taste in the arrangement & decorations of their shops &c. This is particularly observable in the shops of the Milliners, the confectioners and other dealers in fashions and delicacies. The principal streets have a gay look from this circumstance and a stranger is tempted at every turn, to purchase, from the pretty and inviting manner in which the merchandise is spread to view.

 WASHINGTON IRVING
 *Notes and Journal of Travel in Europe*, 17 July 1804

The sensation which France produces on the impression-able foreigner is first of all that of mental exhilaration. Paris, especially, is electric. Touch it at any point and you receive an awakening shock. Live in it and you lose all lethargy. Nothing stagnates. Everyone visibly and acutely feels himself alive. The universal vivacity is con-tagious . . . Nowhere is there so much activity, nowhere so little chaos.

WILLIAM C. BROWNELL
*French Traits*, 1889

Life is almost never in France taken *en amateur*, as it is so largely with us at the present epoch. It is taken, rather, *en connaisseur*.

WILLIAM C. BROWNELL
*French Traits*, 1889

The French have always flattered themselves that they have gone further in the art of living, in what they call *l'entente de la vie*, than any other people.

HENRY JAMES
*Parisian Sketches*

Reading before luncheon. Read that clever amusing book *A Week in a French Country House*. What an ele-gant ease and simplicity there is about French manners and ways of domestic country life, and how favourably it contrasts with our social life, cumbrous, stiff, vulgarly extravagant.

REVD FRANCIS KILVERT
*Diary*, 30 September 1870

It is a liberal education to live in a French provincial town . . . Nowhere else is the way of life more consciously, deliberately, scientifically, made smooth before you. These gentle, happy, kindly, good-tempered, good-mannered people are experts in the Laboratory of Life. Though they seem so ingenuous as to be almost indolent, every action, every impulse, every expression of emotion is calculated, measured, prescribed. Their city is not a fortuitous concourse of incongruous human atoms, but an orderly assembly of men and women inspired by a common purpose. Here is a true community.

JOHN ST LOE STRACHEY
*The River of Life*, 9 October 1922 from Avignon

The last rocket of the fête of July has just mounted, exploded, made a portentous bang, and emitted a gorgeous show of blue-lights . . . The sight which I have just come away from is as brilliant, happy, and beautiful as can be conceived; and if you want to see French people to the greatest advantage, you should go to a festival like this, where their manners, and innocent gaiety, show a very pleasing contrast to the coarse and vulgar hilarity which the same class would exhibit in our own country . . . To me, the prettiest sight was the vast, orderly, happy crowd, the number of children, and the extraordinary care and kindness of the parents towards these little creatures. It does one good to see honest, heavy *épiciers*, fathers of families, playing with them in the Tuileries, or as tonight, bearing them stoutly on their shoulders, through many long hours, in order that the little ones, too, may have their share of the fun.

W.M. THACKERAY
*The Paris Sketch Book*

I returned to England and my school with a knowledge that there existed a land across the water, where everything was different, and delightful, where one walked among marvels, and all food tasted extremely well.

RUDYARD KIPLING, taken to France as
a 12-year-old, reminiscing in
*Souvenirs of France*

The most exquisite diners of all nations say that the French are the most exquisite diners.

WALTER BAGEHOT
'One Difference Between France and England',
*The Economist*, 12 September 1868

Everything ends this way in France – everything. Weddings, christenings, duels, burials, swindlings, diplomatic affairs – everything is a pretext for a good dinner.

JEAN ANOUILH
*Cécile*

In France, cooking is a serious art form and a national sport.

JULIA CHILD

To eat well in France is a universal right – the realistic expectation of the majority, not the privilege of the few.

RAYMOND BLANC

A bad liver is to a Frenchman what a nervous breakdown is to an American. Everyone has had one and everyone wants to talk about it.

ART BUCHWALD

Paris is certainly the culinary centre of the world. Wherever the great cooks are born . . . they all come to Paris to learn their art, and then go out through the whole civilised world as culinary missionaries preaching that there is but one cuisine, and that the Haute Cuisine Française.

LT.-COL. NATHANIEL NEWNHAM-DAVIS
*The Gourmet's Guide to Europe*, 1903

*Mayonnaise, n.* One of the sauces which serve the French in place of a state religion.

AMBROSE BIERCE
*The Devil's Dictionary*

The French palate is the rampart of the most prestigious socio-cultural heritage of humanity and it deserves a more effective fate than the Maginot line.

an editorial in *L'Evènement du Jeudi*
deploring the fall in standards

Our *grande cuisine* existed solely on account of our courtesans.

ROBERT COURTINE
*The Hundred Glories of French Cooking*

We are getting used to tidy, noiseless waiters, who glide hither and thither, and hover about your back and your elbows like butterflies, quick to comprehend orders, quick to fill them; thankful for a gratuity without regard to the amount; and always polite – never otherwise than polite. That is the strangest curiosity yet – a really polite hotel waiter who isn't an idiot.

MARK TWAIN
*The Innocents Abroad*

We have learned to go through the lingering routine of the table d'hôte with patience, with serenity, with satisfaction . . . Wine with every course, of course, being in France. With such a cargo on board, digestion is a slow process, and we must sit long in the cool chambers and smoke.

MARK TWAIN
*The Innocents Abroad*

These three days we have been here, have actually given me an aversion to eating in general . . . What tables we have seen have been so delicately served, and so profusely, that, after rising from one of them, one imagines it impossible ever to eat again.

THOMAS GRAY in Paris
in a letter to Richard West, 12 April 1739

A very modest little dinner at the Café Anglais for two people of long experience, but moderate appetites and limited means, consisted of a dozen Marennes oysters of goodly size and delicious flavour . . .; a *Crécy* soup; *a perdrix aux choux* – a tiny partridge braised with cabbage, carrots, and small sausages; some *gruyère* cheese, a *salade à la romaine*, and a bottle of excellent Bordeaux wine called Pontet Canet. The partridge and cabbage cost ten francs, and the dish was dear at the price; but the Pontet Canet, which cost eight francs, was worth the money, and more, for it was so much purple velvet to the palate . . . This dinner – stay, it included a demi-tasse of coffee and an undeniably authentic Havana cigar . . . – cost twenty-eight francs and some centimes: with the waiter's fee, thirty francs; say twelve shillings a head.

> GEORGE AUGUSTUS SALA
> *Paris Herself Again in 1878–9*

. . . gourmets, eternally engaged in a never-ending search for that imaginary, perfect, unknown little back-street bistro . . .

> ROY ANDRIES DE GROOT
> *Esquire*, May 1970

Let me tell you which is my favourite restaurant in Paris, when I want to dine well and economically. It is a modest little establishment, and nothing whatever to look at from the outside . . . There everything is of the very best: the fish fresher (a tremendous point to gain in Paris), the meat more tender, than at any other restaurant in the town, except the very choicest and most expensive, and its specialty is the roasting of poultry and game. There never was or could be better roasting. And the proprietor, who is also the cook, will serve you, if you like, bread sauce and bread crumbs with our roast game – the most perfect bread sauce imaginable . . . The pheasants, the partridges, the quails, which this beneficent personage puts before you are ever in the choicest condition; and he practically makes you a present of them, for his prices are incredibly low.

> ROWLAND STRONG
> *Where and How to Dine in Paris*, 1900

France today possesses what is probably the most intelligent collective palate.

> M.F.K. FISHER
> *Serve It Forth*

The other day . . . we ate in a garden of the same back street [in Nice] amongst mostly rich peasants and poor medicos – a meal for seven francs . . . An enormous meal . . . unlimited hors d'oeuvres, the best *jambon madère* I have ever eaten; *agneau printanière*; *tomates farcies*; *haricots verts au lard* . . . And drank an interesting little thin, local white wine with a pronounced flavour of *pierre à fusil* – gun flint – and had unlimited soda water and ice with which to dilute it on the hottest day of the year . . . And unlimited melons and pears.

> FORD MADOX FORD
> *Provence*

*La cuisine française* is not one cuisine but a score, regional in origin, shading off into one another at their borders and all pulled together at Paris.

> A.J. LIEBLING
> *Between Meals*

Almost every town of any importance has some special dish or some special pâté of its own, there are hundreds of good old inns where the cuisine is that of the province, and there are great tracks of country, which ought to be marked by some special colour on all guide-book maps, where the cookery is universally good.

> LT.-COL. NATHANIEL NEWNHAM-DAVIS
> *The Gourmet's Guide to Europe*, 1903

The sign says BAR – CRÊPERIE – DÉGUSTATION D'HUÎTRES, and the word *dégustation* means what it says: not 'consumption of' but 'tasting', 'savoring' . . . You are in the country of the art of good food, and this *dégustation* is very like what you do in an art gallery.

ELEANOR CLARK
*The Oysters of Locmariaquer*

*Je me plais infiniment dans ce pays.*

ARNOLD BENNETT
*Journals*, 7 March 1908

At one side there was a table with a row of bottles on it, behind which Madame sat and took the money and made entries in a red book.

KATHERINE MANSFIELD
*An Indiscreet Journey*

Life in the quarter. Our *bistro*, for instance, at the foot of the Hôtel des Trois Moineaux. A tiny brick-floored room, half underground, with wine-sodden tables, and a photograph of a funeral inscribed *'Crédit est mort'*.

GEORGE ORWELL
*Down and Out in Paris and London*

I said to my friends that if I was going to starve, I might as well starve where the food is good.

VIRGIL THOMSON
on life in Paris as a young man

. . . the Taboureau bakery in the rue Turbigo, where the window was filled with all kinds of pastries – *gâteaux aux amandes*, *saint-honorés*, *savarins*, flans and fruit tarts, plates of *babas au rhum*, chocolate éclairs and cream-filled choix, and jars full of macaroons and madeleines.

> EMILE ZOLA
> *Le Ventre de Paris*

We went to France for our holidays and took six large sliced loaves of bread with us. We still had one left after thirteen days. It was still good to eat. This is a tribute to a Leicester bakery.

> a letter in the *Leicester Mercury*
> quoted by Derek Cooper in *The Bad Food Guide*,
> 1967

. . . the somewhat overpoweringly odorous Cheese Department, in which the lordly Camembert, the unpretending but delicious Brie, the milky Bondon, the porous Gruyère, the leather-skinned Port-de-Salut – the last a *fromage pratiquant*, an orthodox cheese, stamped with pious emblems – contend for pre-eminence with the mighty Roquefort – *le fromage qui marche*, as the French significantly call it from its tendency to spontaneous locomotion when kept too long.

> GEORGE AUGUSTUS SALA
> *Paris Herself Again in 1878–9*

I have been in France, and have eaten frogs. The nicest little rabbity things you ever tasted.

> CHARLES LAMB
> in a letter to John Clare

A few years ago, at the Great Gastronomic Parliament in Dijon, a worthy – albeit slightly irresponsible – assembly of chefs undertook to codify the recipe for *coq au vin*.

As if there were only one *coq au vin!*
ROBERT COURTINE
*The Hundred Glories of French Cooking*

In France one's expectations are higher, and one's disappointment at a dull meal consequently greater.
ELIZABETH DAVID
*French Provincial Cooking*

One only eats well at home.
FRENCH SAYING

O, scent of the daubes of my childhood . . . murmuring gently on the stove, giving out sweet smells which brought tears to your eyes. Thyme, rosemary, bay leaves, spices, the wine of the marinade, and the fumet of the meat were becoming transformed . . . into a delicious whole.
PIERRE HUGUENIN
*Les Meilleures Recettes de ma pauvre mère*, 1936

In truth, there is more than carrots and leeks and lump of beef or aged hen in the pot-au-feu; there is a large slice of the heart of France.
ROWLAND STRONG
*Sensations of Paris*, 1912

It is not really an exaggeration to say that peace and happiness begin, geographically, where garlic is used in cooking.
MARCEL BOULESTIN

Having determined to taboo *vin ordinaire* altogether I astonish the *restaurateur* of a village where I take lunch by motioning away the bottle of red wine and calling for *'de l'eau'*, and the glances cast in my direction by the other customers indicate plainly enough that they consider the proceeding as something quite extraordinary.

THOMAS STEVENS
*Around the World on a Bicycle*, 1888

The French drink to get loosened up for an event, to celebrate an event, and even to recover from an event.

GENEVIÈVE GUÉRIN
of the French Commission on Alcoholism, 1980

Other countries drink to get drunk . . . ; in France, drunkenness is a consequence, never an intention. A drink is had to prolong a pleasure . . . wine is not only a philtre but the leisurely act of drinking.

ROLAND BARTHES
*Mythologies*, 'Wine and Milk'

The wine commonly drank at Boulogne comes from Auxerre, is very small and meagre, and may be had from five to eight sols a bottle; that is, from two-pence half-penny to four-pence. The French inhabitants drink no good wine; nor is there any to be had, unless you have recourse to the British wine-merchants here established, who deal in Bourdeaux wines, brought hither by sea for the London market. I have very good claret from a friend, at the rate of fifteen-pence sterling a bottle; and excellent small beer as reasonable as in England.

TOBIAS SMOLLETT
*Travels through France and Italy*, 1766

*Pastis* time?

The Channel Tunnel. The train stops for the third time.
*Passenger:* 'Where are we now, Guard?'
From *Punch* in 1907

We . . . vomited as usual into the Channel which divides Albion from Gallia. Rivers are said to run blood after an engagement; the Channel is discoloured, I am sure, in a less elegant and less pernicious way by English tourists going and coming.

REVD SIDNEY SMITH
in a letter to Sir Wilmot-Horton, December 1835

Passage to Calais; fourteen hours for reflection in a vehicle that does not allow one power to reflect.

ARTHUR YOUNG
*Travels in France*, 1792

I Was never before so Sea sick, nor was my Son. My Servant was very bad. Allmost all the Passengers were sick. It is a remarkable Place for it.

JOHN ADAMS
*Diary*, 23 October 1783

A tunnel underneath the sea, from Calais, straight to
    Dover, Sir,
That qualmish folks may cross by land from shore to
    shore . . .
Has long been talked of, till at length 'tis thought a
    *monstrous bore*.

THEODORE HOOK
*Bubbles of 1825*

We left Dover at twelve at noon, and with a pretty brisk gale, which pleased everybody mighty well, except myself, who was extremely sick the whole time: we reached Calais by five . . . Calais is an exceeding old, but very pretty town, and we hardly saw any thing there that was not so new and so different from England, that it surprised us agreeably.

THOMAS GRAY
in a letter to his mother from Amiens, 1 April 1739

There is . . . something very pleasing in the manners and appearance of the people of Calais, that prepossesses you in their favour. A national reflection might occur, that when Edward III took Calais, he turned out the old inhabitants, and peopled it almost entirely with our own countrymen; but unfortunately the manners are not English.

MARY SHELLEY
*History of a Six Weeks' Tour*, 29 July 1814

I like Boulogne very much it is a pretty lively place always plenty of life going on and you can have a ball any night you please they dance every night . . . Steamers arrive here every day from London and Folkestone with lots of passengers though the hotels are so crammed full that they had to send out for matrasses for beds and the travellers had to sleep in the dining-room, what a mania some years there is for a place and it is crammed fuller than it can hold.

MARIE LOUISE DE LA RAMÉE (OUIDA)
*Journal*, 3 August 1850, when she was eleven

. . . a large, old, fortified town, with more English in it than French.

THOMAS GRAY of Boulogne
in a letter to his mother from Amiens, 1 April 1739

Boulogne and back.
From *Punch* in 1899

The shop-keepers here drive a considerable traffic with the English smugglers, whose cutters are almost the only vessels one sees in the harbour of Boulogne . . . The smugglers from the coast of Kent and Sussex pay English gold for great quantities of French brandy, tea, coffee, and small wine, which they run from this country. They likewise buy glass trinkets, toys, and coloured prints, which sell in England, for no other reason, but that they come from France, as they may be had as cheap, and much better finished, of our own manufacture. They likewise take off ribbons, laces, linen and cambrics . . . I have made a provision of shirts for one half of the money they would have cost in London.

TOBIAS SMOLLETT
*Travels through France and Italy*, 1766

I began as I meant to go on: sitting in the sun before the Café des Tribunaux in Dieppe in company with a litre of Provençal Rosé, a crisp loaf, a slice of oozing cheese and strawberries.

TOM VERNON
*Fat Man on a Bicycle*

At 10.30 we went off in our car . . . to Amiens. We went through Abbeville and Picquigny. No possible restaurant at Picquigny, or at Ailly – nothing indeed between Abbeville and Amiens. Relative barbarism of French provincial towns (*pavé*, etc, dullness). We had a fine lunch at the Petit Vatel. Rather disappointed with the Cathedral – except the West Front. Some lovely bits of architecture in the town.

ARNOLD BENNETT
*Journals*, 9 July 1928

The roads are not only planted with trees, but in some places, for miles, are in straight lines, which is not very pleasant. They go on in a line from one village to another, so that when we leave one we immediately see the church of another at the extremity of the vista.

> DR EDWARD RIGBY in French Flanders
> *Letters from France in 1789*

Long straight lines of poplars delight the French; they suit the military turn of the nation.

> T.J. HOGG
> *Two Hundred and Nine Days on the Continent,* 1827

Amiens, Montreuil and Clermont the only pleasant places till we came to Chantilly and the plains of St Denis; I then thought it fairy-land. The plantations are beautiful, and for many miles you ride in an avenue. The almond trees and fruit trees in the fields greatly enriched the scene.

> LADY KNIGHT
> in a letter, 17 April 1776

The chief charm of Trouville, the lovely winding road along the coast to the mouth of the Seine at Honfleur, called the 'Corniche Normande', because it is, if anything, more beautiful than the famous 'Route de la Corniche' at Cannes, has also been spoilt by innumerable automobiles driven at frantic speed by arrogant and cosmopolitan parvenus. Villerville, between Trouville and Honfleur, is far prettier, and, though cheaper, attracts a better class of visitor.

> ROWLAND STRONG
> *Sensations of Paris,* 1912

Normandy has a bad reputation for rain and on that account is called the *pot de chambre* of France.
R.H. BRUCE-LOCKHART
*My Europe*, 1952

The blues and browns of Brittany are sorrowful and watery. Picardy is cold and prim in yellowish grey. In lush Normandy the pastures are as green velvet, while the Norman chalk dunes have the rich friable whiteness of cream cheese.
ROWLAND STRONG
*Sensations of Paris*, 1912

There is one sight which every gastronome sees with pleasure at Mont St Michel, and that is the making of the great eighteen egg omelet at the restaurant of Poulard Ainé. It is quite a function, and the skill with which the omelet is transferred from the pan to the dish is to be noticed appreciatively.
LT.-COL. NATHANIEL NEWNHAM-DAVIS
*The Gourmet's Guide to Europe*, 1903

Brittany, the land of butter and eggs . . . Roscoff is celebrated for its *primeurs*, for the Gulf Stream gives it an equable climate, and the market gardeners whose ground is near the sea supply vegetables to the Paris markets very early in the year. Lobsters and *langoustes* are exported in great quantities from Roscoff, and here, as along all the Brittany coast, prawns, artichokes, eggs, lobsters, crabs, *langoustes* are plentiful.
LT.-COL. NATHANIEL NEWNHAM-DAVIS
*The Gourmet's Guide to Europe*, 1903

There is nothing to be learned by travelling in France. I can say this from my own experience. So what I propose and insist on is that you come directly . . . to Paris, which as the metropolis of France is worth while to say you have seen, and which you may see fully in three or four days.

LORD AUCHINLECK
in a letter to his son James Boswell, 10 August 1765

Approached Paris, Invalides appeared as St Paul's does, coming to London. Was not affected much.

JAMES BOSWELL
*Journal*, 12 January 1766

I cannot tell you what an immense impression Paris made upon me. It is the most extraordinary place in the world . . . I cannot conceive any place so perfectly and wonderfully expressive of its own character.

CHARLES DICKENS
in a letter to the Comte d'Orsay, 7 August 1844

There were also, if one had made the necessary economies, celestial gingerbreads to be bought everywhere.

RUDYARD KIPLING in Paris as a 12-year-old
*Souvenirs of France*

Paris is the place in the world where, if you wish, you may best unite the *utile* and the *dulce*.

LORD CHESTERFIELD
in a letter, 30 April 1750

'Fumeurs, M'sieur?'
'Non, non – *Paris*.'
From *Punch* in 1906

Paris is not so fine a place as you would expect. The palaces and churches, however, are very splendid and magnificent; and . . . there are many fine pictures; but I do not think their way of life commodious or pleasant.

DR SAMUEL JOHNSON
in a letter to Mrs Lucy Porter, 16 November 1775

Paris, where you can get a sight of it, is really fine. The view from the bridges is even more imposing and picturesque than ours . . . The clearness of the air, the glittering sunshine, and the cool shadows add to the enchantment of the scene. In a bright day it dazzles the eye like a steel mirror . . . Paris is a splendid vision, a fabric dug out of the earth, and hanging over it.

WILLIAM HAZLITT
*Notes of a Journey through France and Italy*, 1826

We visited the church of Notre Dame, a very beautiful Gothic building . . . From the top of this church we had a complete bird's-eye view of Paris, not so large as London, but the buildings being of stone, and white, the effect is more striking. We have now seen enough of Paris to be convinced that it is not that dirty, ill-built, inconvenient place, which our ill-tempered countrymen have described it. There are more magnificent buildings than in London; all the places worth seeing are likewise more accessible than in London; it costs less to be admitted, and many may be seen without paying anything.

DR EDWARD RIGBY in Paris
*Letters from France in 1789*

My eyes do not grow weary in gazing at this Paris, so full of marvels; Paris, the City of Light, as Victor Hugo called it with such truth, beyond dispute the most beautiful of all cities.

> SIR WILFRED LAURIER
> Canadian prime minister, in an address
> in Paris, August 1897

Paris is a great beauty. As such it possesses all the qualities that one finds in any other great beauty; chic, sexiness, grandeur, arrogance.

> FRAN LEBOWITZ
> *Metropolitan Life*

France is a man, Paris is the heart.

> KING HENRI IV

The heart of France beats in Paris, and the excessive centralisation of the French has centred the hopes and ambitions in their capital.

> SIR WILLIAM CLAYTON
> *Journals* 1861–1914

France is *l'homme sensuel moyen*, the average sensual man; Paris is the city of *l'homme sensuel moyen*.    This has an attraction for all of us.

> MATTHEW ARNOLD
> *Literature and Dogma*

. . . the patrimony of all mankind.

> JOHN VINOCUR on Paris
> *New York Times*, March 1985

Paris rawly waking, crude sunlight on her lemon streets.
JAMES JOYCE
*Ulysses*

Old, crumbling walls and the pleasant sound of water running in the urinals.
HENRY MILLER

The best of America drifts to Paris. The American in Paris is the best American. It is more fun for an intelligent person to live in an intelligent country. France has the only two things toward which we drift as we grow older – intelligence and good manners.
F. SCOTT FITZGERALD
*New York World*, April 1927

Alice deplores the public urinals. I keep explaining to Alice that the Parisians are all wine-drinkers and for a gentleman the bladder is more restless than for a lady.
GERTRUDE STEIN

If I were to choose one single thing that would restore Paris to the senses, it would be that strangely sweet, unhealthy smell of the Métro, so very unlike the dank cold or the stuffy heat of subways in New York.
MAY SARTON
*I Knew a Phoenix*, 1959

The ample proportions of the Boulevard are necessary to the Parisian for his gesticulations, and for the breadth of his ideas on moral, social, and political topics . . . The Boulevard is the throat of Paris, and its palate as well.
ROWLAND STRONG
*Sensations of Paris*, 1912

The Boulevard de Sébastopol in Paris, in 1859

Paris appears to be a vast temple of pleasure; the whole population turning out at even-tide *pour s'amuser*; and such a sight as the Champs Elysées near us exhibits by lamplight can be seen nowhere else . . . The very business of Parisian existence appears to be pleasure, whereas the truest pleasure of London seems to be business: never was there such a contrast. But really I take it there is a great amount of merely childish innocent amusement in Paris gaiety: London may have sterner duties and guiltier pleasures.

MARTIN F. TUPPER
*Paterfamilias' Diary of Everybody's Tour*, 1856

I do not know anything . . . more wonderful than the sight of the thousands of well-dressed people who sit all day, and during a great portion of the night, in and outside the boulevard cafés, smoking, drinking, playing at cards and dominoes, and otherwise enjoying themselves.

GEORGE AUGUSTUS SALA
*Paris Herself Again in 1878–9*

We went to a restaurant, just after lamplighting, and ate a comfortable, satisfactory, lingering dinner. It was a pleasure to eat where everything was so tidy, the food so well cooked, the waiters so polite, and the coming and departing company so moustached, so frisky, so affable, so fearfully and wonderfully Frenchy! All the surroundings were gay and enlivening. Two hundred people sat at little tables on the sidewalk, sipping wine and coffee; the streets were thronged with light vehicles and with joyous pleasure-seekers.

MARK TWAIN
*The Innocents Abroad*

Of all the great cities, Paris is the most tolerable in hot weather. It is true that the asphalt has a way of liquefying to about the consistency and the temperature of molten lava . . . But . . . the boulevards are a long chain of cafés, each one with its little promontory of chairs and tables projecting into the sea of asphalt . . . Then you may dine in the Champs Elysées at a table spread under the trees, beside an ivied wall, and almost believe you are in the country.

> HENRY JAMES
> *Parisian Sketches*

The café of Europe.
ABBÉ GALIANI

The Champs Elysées at 10 p.m.

Here nobody sleeps; it is not the way.
  THOMAS GRAY


They crossed the Place de la Concorde as only
Frenchmen can; that is to say they sauntered through the
traffic chatting away, looking neither to right nor to left.
  NANCY MITFORD
  *The Blessing*


Paris is eloquent.  Above the multifarious noises of the
street, which are of a mechanical origin, . . . there con-
stantly arises the wail of protestation, the yell of denunci-
atory wrath.  Two Paris drivers collide with each other, or
narrowly escape a collision.  *'Ours!'* (Bear!) shouts one.
*'Fourneau!'* (Fire-stove!) bellows the other.  If damage
has been done, a policeman intervenes.
  ROWLAND STRONG
  *Sensations of Paris*, 1912


I know Baron Haussman made Paris a grand place to look
at, but the man had no concept of traffic flow. At the
Arc de Triomphe alone thirteen roads come together.
  BILL BRYSON
  *Neither Here Nor There*


. . . that screaming wolf pack of fast traffic that is more
terrifying, more concentratedly breathless, more egotisti-
cal, more ravening after human prey than any other
traffic in Europe.
  V.S. PRITCHETT writing in 1963
  *At Home and Abroad*

The shops are splendid, and for show, pleasure, and luxury this place is . . . the capital of Europe; and as Europe gets richer and richer, and show, pleasure, and luxury are more and more valued, Paris will be more and more important, and more and more the capital of Europe.

MATTHEW ARNOLD
in a letter to his mother, 12 April 1865

The window of a Parisian shop . . . is a sight worth going a day's journey to witness; it is quite a study – a perfect picture. It affords an exhibition of artistical skill of which the people of no other country can have any conception.

JAMES GRANT
*Paris and its People*, 1843

Paris is the place in the world where one can be poor with the least privation; it is only the tiresome and the foolish who require to be rich.

JULIE DE LESPINASSE
in a letter, 19 September 1774

Paris *should* be walked, because much of it, the most secret, the most modest, the most bizarre, the tiniest, is only discoverable by the pedestrian who is prepared to push behind the boulevards and the long straight streets of the Second Empire.

RICHARD COBB
*The Streets of Paris*

Paris, besides being a beautiful city in the quarter that strangers most look to, . . . delights the eye of a man of letters by the multitude of its book-stalls . . . I thought, if I were a bachelor, not an Englishman, and had no love for old friends and fields, and no decided religious opinions, I could live very well, for the rest of my life, in a lodging above one of the booksellers' shops in the Quai de Voltaire, where I should look over the water to the Tuileries, and have the Elysian fields in my eye for my evening walk.

LEIGH HUNT
*Autobiography*

Four hours more at the Louvre, that exhaustless mine of art and interest: in paintings and sculpture at all events most other collections pale beside it.

MARTIN F. TUPPER
*Paterfamilias' Diary of Everybody's Tour*, 1856

As an artist, a man has no home in Europe save in Paris.

FRIEDRICH NIETZSCHE
*Ecce Homo*

There is but one Paris and however hard living may be here, . . . – the French air clears up the brain and does good – a world of good.

VINCENT VAN GOGH
in a letter to an English artist
considering moving to Paris, summer 1886

In Paris life passes like a dream.

FRENCH PROVERB

Paradoxically, the freedom of Paris is associated with a persistent belief that nothing ever changes. After an absence of twenty or thirty years, one still recognizes it.

MARGUERITE DURAS

Versailles! It is wonderfully beautiful! You gaze and stare and try to understand that it is real, that it is on the earth, that it is not the Garden of Eden . . . I know now that the pictures never came up to the subject in any respect, and that no painter could represent Versailles on canvas as beautiful as it is in reality. I used to abuse Louis XIV for spending two hundred millions of dollars in creating this marvelous park when bread was so scarce with some of his subjects, but I have forgiven him now.

MARK TWAIN
*The Innocents Abroad*

Well! and is this the great front of Versailles? What a huge heap of littleness!

THOMAS GRAY
in a letter, May 1739

There are a dozen country houses of private individuals in England alone which have a greater air of majesty and splendour than this huge quarry.

T.B. MACAULAY on Versailles
*Journal*, 2 February 1839

A day at Versailles: warned by the tedium of guide-books, one really dare not detail it: all the world is well enough aware of its square miles of immense historical pictures, chiefly the battles of Napoleon . . . For five hours – and therefore for almost twice as many miles – we slided on those perilous polished floors through suites of gilded rooms crowded with history on canvas.

MARTIN F. TUPPER
*Paterfamilias' Diary of Everybody's Tour*, 1856

Monkish-looking priests are a characteristic feature of these villages, and when, on passing down the narrow, crooked streets of Fontenay, I wheel beneath a massive stone archway, and looking around, observe cowled priests and everything about the place seemingly in keeping with it, one can readily imagine himself transported back to medieval times. One of these little interior French villages is the most unpromising looking place imaginable for a hungry person to ride into; often one may ride the whole length of the village expectantly looking around for some visible evidence of wherewith to cheer the inner man, and all that greets the hungry vision is a couple of four-foot sticks of bread in one dust-begrimed window, and a few mournful-looking crucifixes and Roman Catholic paraphernalia in another.

THOMAS STEVENS east of Paris
*Around the World on a Bicycle*, 1888

If you want information in the villages of France, find an old woman. They know everything, and they love to talk.

ROBERT DALEY
*Portraits of France*

The streets in general have but a melancholy aspect, the houses all old . . . What pleasures the place denies to the sight, it makes up to the palate, since you have nothing to drink but the best champagne in the world, and all sort of provisions equally good.

THOMAS GRAY in Rheims
in a letter to his mother, 21 June 1739

Every French town has an Avenue Victor Hugo.

BARBARA TUCHMAN

The château is the one thing to be seen at *la Fontaine de belle eau*, and we have just done our touristical devoir thereby. It is a mixture of splendour and shabbiness, a wilderness of gilded rooms approached by mean passages and common staircases; without its historical interests, Francis and Henry and Louis, Marie-Antoinette, Pio Septimo and Napoleon, there is not much to stop the traveller.

MARTIN F. TUPPER at Fontainebleau
*Paterfamilias' Diary of Everybody's Tour*, 1856

Azay is a most perfect and beautiful thing; I should place it third in any list of the great houses of this part of France in which these houses should be ranked according to charm. For beauty of detail it comes after Blois and Chenonceaux; but it comes before Amboise and Chambord. On the other hand, of course, it is inferior in majesty to either of these vast structures. Like Chenonceaux, it is a watery place, though it is more meagrely moated than the little château on the Cher.

HENRY JAMES
*A Little Tour in France*, 1884

Touraine, the garden of France.

FRANÇOIS RABELAIS

We have come five hundred miles by rail through the heart of France. What a bewitching land it is! – what a garden! Surely the leagues of bright green lawns are swept and brushed and watered every day, and their grasses trimmed by the barber. Surely the hedges are shaped and measured, and their symmetry preserved, by the most architectural of gardeners. Surely the long straight rows of stately poplars that divide the beautiful landscape like the squares of a chequer-board are set with line and plummet, and their uniform height determined with a spirit level. Surely the straight, smooth, pure white turnpikes are jackplaned and sandpapered every day. How else are these marvels of symmetry, cleanliness and order attained! It is wonderful. There are no unsightly stone walls, and never a fence of any kind. There is no dirt, no decay, no rubbish anywhere.

MARK TWAIN
*The Innocents Abroad*, 1869

Every French road has a touch of despotism in it.
ANTHONY TROLLOPE

The joys of touring in France: straight roads, smooth as a racing track, but an unobtrusive ditch outside every village. From *Punch* in 1907

Queer old towns, draw-bridged and walled: with odd little
towers at the angles, like grotesque faces, as if the wall
had put a mask on, and were staring, down into the moat;
other strange little towers, in gardens and fields, and
down lanes, and in farmyards: all alone, and always
round, with a peaked roof, and never used for any purpose
at all; ruinous buildings of all sorts: sometimes an hôtel de
ville, sometimes a guard-house, sometimes a château with
a rank garden, prolific in dandelion, and watched over by
extinguisher-topped turrets, and blink-eyed little case-
ments; are the standard objects, repeated over and over
again.

> CHARLES DICKENS
> on the road between Paris and Chalon-sur-Saône
> *Pictures from Italy*

On my way to this town [Beaune] I passed the stretch of
the Côte d'Or, which, covered with a mellow autumn
haze, with the sunshine shimmering through, looked
indeed like a golden slope. One regards with a kind of
awe the region in which the famous crûs of Burgundy
(Vougeot, Chambertin, Nuits, Beaune) are, I was going
to say, manufactured.

> HENRY JAMES
> *A Little Tour in France*

Spring that year was remarkably mild . . . and in
Clochemerle drinking at the summer rhythm started in
May . . . The result was that the men's kidneys were
working full out, and the closeness of the urinal to the
inn made it a popular destination.

> GABRIEL CHEVALLIER
> *Clochemerle*

*Guide:* 'Monsieur finds eet vairy eenteresting?'
*Harry:* 'Pas demi!'
    From *Punch* in 1906

The French never allow a distinguished son of France to lack a statue.

> E.V. LUCAS
> *Wanderings and Diversions*, 1926

It is market morning. The market is held in the little square outside, in front of the cathedral. It is crowded with men and women, in blue, in red, in green, in white; with canvassed stalls; and fluttering merchandise. The country people are grouped about, with their clean baskets before them.

> CHARLES DICKENS in Chalon-sur-Saône
> *Pictures from Italy*

Every morning I go to the market and wander about among the stalls. This is a Lyonnais tradition which I find hard to abandon . . . I know that one stallholder will have the best artichokes, another particularly good spinach . . .

> PAUL BOCUSE
> *The Cuisine of Paul Bocuse*

Picnics in France combine so many joys. First, the buying, to be done as often as possible in a market rather than in shops.

> ELIZABETH DAVID
> *An Omelette and a Glass of Wine*

The ham of Bayonne, the *pâté de foie gras* of Périgueux, you bury in the deep recesses of a long, narrow, crisp *petit pain*, and then, quick in a French railway carriage will you find yourself: a bottle of wine is at your side.

> ELIZABETH ROBINS PENNELL
> *A Guide for the Greedy*, 1923

From Puits d'Or to Lyons the scenery was picturesque beyond description . . . The approach to Lyons is uncommonly beautiful, with such a multitude of châteaux and country houses, belonging to the rich manufacturers of the city, of farm-houses and neat cottages, all commanding beautiful prospects, as is perhaps not to be equalled in any part of the world.

> DR EDWARD RIGBY
> *Letters from France in 1789*

The rents are so low, and provisions so astonishingly cheap round Lyons, that this gentleman assured me a person with a wife and a small family might live well for sixty pounds a year. What a charming country this is, for people of small fortunes! There are many English families settled here.

> DR EDWARD RIGBY
> *Letters from France in 1789*

Certain it is, my dear Madam, that everything is reasonable here.

> LADY KNIGHT
> in a letter from Toulouse, 6 October 1776

We found plenty of good mutton, pork, poultry, and game, including the red partridge, which is near twice as big as the partridge of England. Their hares are likewise surprisingly large and juicy. We saw great flocks of black turkeys feeding in the fields, but no black cattle; and milk was so scarce, that sometimes we were obliged to drink our tea without it.

> TOBIAS SMOLLETT
> *Travels through France and Italy*, 5 November 1763

In Dordogne there is not a peasant who cannot give a traveller *en panne* a truffled omelette which would make an alderman's mouth water.

> LT.-COL. NATHANIEL NEWNHAM-DAVIS
> *The Gourmet's Guide to Europe*, 1903

In the store room next to the kitchen were a long table and shelves always covered with all sorts of provisions; large earthenware jars full of *confits* of pork and goose, a small barrel where vinegar slowly matured, a bowl where honey oozed out of the comb, jams, preserves of sorrel and of tomatoes, and odd bottles with grapes and cherries marinating in brandy; . . . sacks of haricot beans, of potatoes; eggs, each one carefully dated in pencil.

And there were the baskets of fruit, perfect small melons, late plums, under-ripe medlars waiting to soften, peaches, pears hollowed out by a bird or wasp, figs that had fallen of their own accord, all the fruits of September naturally ripe and sometimes still warm from the sun. Everything in profusion.

> MARCEL BOULESTIN remembering his
> grandmother's kitchen at St Aulaye in the Périgord
> *Myself, My Two Countries*

. . . pour into the soup a quarter of a litre of red wine and drink the whole from the bowl . . . This fashion of lapping it up is called by the men of the South-West *faire Chabrol*. No one seems to know why.

> ALAN HOUGHTON-BRODRICK
> *Cross-Channel*

Bordeaux is a big, rich, handsome, imposing commercial town, with long rows of fine old eighteenth-century houses, which overlook the yellow Garonne . . . The appearance of such a port as this makes the Anglo-Saxon tourist blush for the sordid water-fronts of Liverpool and New York, which, with their larger activity, have so much more reason to be stately. Bordeaux gives a great impression of prosperous industries, and suggests delightful ideas, images of prune-boxes and claret. As the focus of distribution of the best wine in the world, it is indeed a sacred city – dedicated to the worship of Bacchus in the most discreet form.

> HENRY JAMES
> *A Little Tour in France*, 1884

. . . a city built almost entirely on wine.

> ROBERT DALEY
> *Portraits of France*

The French '*dame du comptoir*' has a keen scent for unprofitable customers, which the '*garçon*' soon discerns – the habitués who sit long and order nothing.

> SIR WILLIAM CLAYTON
> *Journals 1861–1914*

By Carcassonne they have already begun to use a little pork-fat . . . But it is not until you get to Castelnaudary – of the *cassoulets* – that cooking with goose-fat begins, and *foie gras* and truffles and the real *haute cuisine* of the Toulousain district and the real, high wines of the Bordelais.

> FORD MADOX FORD
> *Provence*

Every place has its favourite dishes
And boasts of its special delights:
La Grasse has its plump partridges,
Villasavarry its luscious melons,
Limoux its sparkling *blanquette*,
Albi gilds its pastry rings.
All towns have some crowning glory,
But Castelnaudary alone has the cassoulet.
    refrain of the local *Canson d'el cassoulet*

I want to take you to *Chez Clémence*, a small bistro in the rue Vavin, where only one dish is made, but a prodigious one. It is well known that in order to develop its full flavour cassoulet must simmer only on low heat. Mère Clémence's cassoulet has been cooking for twenty years. She adds to the pot, from time to time, some goose, pork fat, perhaps a piece of saucisson or a few beans. But it is always the same cassoulet: the base remains the same.
    ANATOLE FRANCE
    *Histoire comique*

The auberge of Bouchet St Nicolas was among the least pretentious I have ever visited; but I saw many more of the like upon my journey. Indeed, it was typical of these French highlands. Imagine a cottage of two storeys, with a bench before the door; the stable and kitchen in a *suite*, so that Modestine and I could hear each other dining; furniture of the plainest, earthern floors, a single bed-chamber for travellers, and that without any convenience but beds. In the kitchen cooking and eating go forward side by side, and the family sleep at night. Any one who

has a fancy to wash must do so in public at the common table. The food is sometimes spare; hard fish and omelette have been my portion more than once; . . .and the visit of a fat sow, grouting under the table and rubbing against your legs, is no impossible accompaniment to dinner.

ROBERT LOUIS STEVENSON
*Travels with a Donkey in the Cévennes*

Vaour is a village I don't know how many miles off Fenayrols. I only know that we went there, and it lies eleven kilometres from a railway station. The Hôtel du Nord at Vaour is illustrious throughout the region for its cookery. People travel vast distances uphill in order to enjoy it. We did. We arrived at eleven o'clock and lunch was just ending. The landlord and landlady in the kitchen said that we were unfortunately too late for a proper meal, but they would see what they could do for us. Here is what they did for us: *Soupe, Jambon du pays, Confit d'Oie, Omelette nature, Civet de lièvre, Riz de veau blanquette, Perdreau rôti, Fromage Roquefort, Fromage Cantal, Confiture de cerises, Poires, Figues.* We ate everything; every dish was really distinguished . . . In addition, there were three wines. The total bill, for two persons, was seven francs.

ARNOLD BENNETT
*Things that Have Interested Me*

I came once more in sight of some red windows. This time they were differently disposed. It was not *Fouzilhic*, but *Fouzilhac*, a hamlet little distant from the other in space, but worlds away in the spirit of its inhabitants.

ROBERT LOUIS STEVENSON
*Travels with a Donkey in the Cévennes*

85

There is a certain little meadow by the sea, under Mount Canigou, which Spring fills with narcissi when she first sets foot in Europe. For years in succession we went down to that meadow, spread our maps among the flowers, and began our travels – all France to play with, and our auto to convey us. From the tourists' point of view March is not a good season. Winds blow . . Yet, for those who love the land and its people, March is the month above all; for then France, who never stops working, begins her spring cleanings, loppings, and prunings.

> RUDYARD KIPLING
> *Souvenirs of France*

There is an inexhaustible sweetness in the grey-green landscape of Provence. It is never absolutely flat, and yet is never really ambitious, and is full both of entertainment and repose. It is in constant undulation, and the bareness of the soil lends itself to outline and profile. When I say the bareness, I mean the absence of woods and hedges. It blooms with heath and scented shrubs and stunted olive; and the white rock shining through the scattered herbage has a brightness which answers to the brightness of the sky.

> HENRY JAMES
> *A Little Tour in Fance*, 1884

. . . Blazing lights, red earth, blue sea, mauve twilight, the flake of gold buried in the black depths of the cypress; archaic tastes of wine and olive, ancient smells of dust, goat dung and thyme, immemorial sounds of cicada and rustic flute.

> ROBERT HUGHES
> on Provence, *Time*, October 1984

Avignon is remarkable for the number seven; having seven ports, seven parishes, seven colleges, seven hospitals, and seven monasteries; and I may add, I think, seven hundred bells, which are always making a horrid jingle; for they have no idea of ringing bells harmoniously in any part of France.

> PHILIP THICKNESSE
> *A Year's Journey through France and Spain*, 1789

I think it wrong, merely because a man's hat has been blown off his head by chance the first night he comes to Avignon – that he should therefore say, 'Avignon is more subject to high winds than any town in all France'; for which reason I laid no stress upon the accident till . . . hearing the windiness of Avignon spoke of in the country about as a proverb, I set it down, merely to ask the learned what can be the cause.

> LAURENCE STERNE
> *Tristram Shandy*

The *mistral* is *agaçant*.

> ARNOLD BENNETT
> *Journals*, 10 March 1924, from Avignon

. . . a harsh philistine wind.

> OSCAR WILDE
> in a letter to Reginald Turner, 3 January 1899

. . . which blows relentlessly, with no obstacles in its path, and seems to flatten the countryside, increasing its feeling of solitude and immensity.

> ALPHONSE DAUDET on the Camargue
> *Lettres de mon moulin*

And so I have seen the immortal Pont du Gard. It is the least disappointing sight I have ever beheld . . . In spite of the endless photographs, engravings, and 'cuts' in every book of architecture ever attempted, it utterly surprised me with its majesty and yet absolute appropriateness and moderation.

JOHN ST LOE STRACHEY
*The River of Life*, 15 October 1922

It looks as though it had been built long before all record by beings greater than ourselves, and were intended to stand long after the dissolution of our petty race. One can repose in it.

HILAIRE BELLOC
*Many Cities*

It is a Roman triumph of the plumbers' science.

LAWRENCE DURRELL
*Spirit of Place*

The Provençal character is the most many-sided that can be found – a character founded on shrewdness, frugality, and infinite pawky knowledge of the vicissitudes that beset human lives.

FORD MADOX FORD
*Provence*

To attempt to speed things up in Provence is but a further waste of time and energy.

WINIFRED LADY FORTESCUE
*Perfume from Provence*

Before eight o'clock I was down in the village with my *filet* in my hand a-getting of the lunch and the dinner. And although it pleuvéd cats and dogs I marched about the land, and came back home a kind of hardened sinner.
*For* the *petits pois*, I really must confess,
Were sinfully expensive and I couldn't have bought
     less.
I *had* to buy a *demi-livre*, and that's by no means
     ample.
By the time that they've been shelled and cooked, *il ne
     reste plus qu'un* sample.

KATHERINE MANSFIELD
*Journal*, March 1916, at Bandol in the Var

By day the cicadas are inaudible in the rattle of typewriters, by night the glow-worms are upstaged by the flicker of VDUs, for the hills are alive with the sound of expatriate hacks shrieking that they could be the next Peter Mayle.

ALAN COREN on Provence
writing in *The Times*, May 1993

We had a most delicious journey to Marselles through a Country sweetely declining to the South & Mediterranean Coasts, full of Vine-yards, & Olive-yards, Orange Trees, Myrtils, Pomegranads & the like sweete Plantations, to which belong innumerable pleasantly situated Villas, to the number of above fifteen hundred; built all of Freestone, and most of them in prospect shewing as if they were so many heapes of snow dropp'd out of the clowds amongst those perennial greenes.

JOHN EVELYN
*Diary*, October 1644


The peculiarity of the appearance of the landscape is, I believe, that at a little distance everything seems translucent. You seem to see the light of the sky *through* the mountains . . . There are no lines only gradation of colour on colour.

Let no one tell me I am in the nineteenth century, nothing of the kind. Nothing later, at all events, than the conquests of the Saracens. But rather I am in times long before that. These are the mountains that the Greek colonists saw. The sea and the shore having nothing altered since the times when Carthage was the great Empire of the Mediterranean.

The end of October, and here I bask in delicious sunshine! I write and read on the open deck . . . The sun is just setting over one of the little Ile d'Hières. Westward, all the mountains about Marseilles and Toulon are bathed, etherealized in a light half yellow, half purple. To the east, the sky is growing a darker purple and the land of the same colour. My first Mediterranean sunset!

GEORGE GISSING
in a letter to his sister Ellen, 28 October 1888

Eat *bouillabaisse* in Marseilles . . . the saffron's gold has richer tone, the *ail's* aroma sweeter savour, under hot blue southern skies than in the cold sunless north . . .

Walk out in the early morning on the quays; the summer sky is cloudless; the sea as blue as in the painter's bluest dream; the hills but warm purple shadows resting upon its waters. The air is hot, perhaps, but soft and dry, and the breeze blows fresh from over the Mediterranean. Already, on every side, signs there are of the day's coming sacrifice. In sunlight and in shadow are piled high the sea's sweetest, choicest fruits: mussels in their sombre purple shells; lobsters, rich and brown, fish, scarlet and gold and green. Lemons, freshly plucked from near gardens, are scattered among the fragrant pile, and here and there trail long sprays of salt, pungent seaweed. The faint smell of *ail* comes to you gently from unseen kitchens, the feeling of *bouillabaisse* is everywhere . . .

ELIZABETH ROBINS PENNELL
*A Guide for the Greedy*, 1923

If you do not like oil, garlic, and saffron, which all come into its composition, give it a wide berth.

LT.-COL. NATHANIEL NEWNHAM-DAVIS
*The Gourmet's Guide to Europe*, 1903

I know of nothing more appetising, on a very hot day, than to sit down in the cool shade of a dining-room with drawn Venetian blinds, at a little table laid with black olives, *saucisson d'Arles*, some fine tomatoes, a slice of water melon and a pyramid of little green figs baked by the sun. One will scarcely resist the pleasure of afterwards tasting the anchovy tart or the roast of lamb

The Francophile's Quotation Book

cooked on the spit, its skin perfectly browned, or the dish of tender little artichokes in oil . . . The midi is essentially a region of carefully prepared little dishes.

MME LÉON DAUDET writing as 'Pampille'
*Les Bons Plats de France*

When I stand upon the rampart, and look round me, I can scarce help thinking myself inchanted. The small extent of country which I see, is all cultivated like a garden. Indeed, the plain presents nothing but gardens, full of green trees, loaded with oranges, lemons, citrons, and bergamots, which make a delightful appearance . . . and plates of roses, carnations, ranunculas, anemonies, and daffodils, blowing in full glory, with such beauty, vigour, and perfume, as no flower in England ever exhibited.

TOBIAS SMOLLET in Nice
*Travels through France and Italy*, 15 January 1764

This place is so wonderfully dry that nothing can be kept moist . . . There is some water in the sea, but not much . . . It is a queer place – Brighton and Belgravia and Baden by the Mediterranean: odious to me in all respects but its magnificent winter climate.

EDWARD LEAR on Nice
in a letter to Chichester Fortescue,
24 February 1865

Christmas time was usually golden and warm. We ate out on the terrace sometimes, always drank our *kir royale* outside, admired the early marigolds and anemones, rejoiced at the sharp green thrusts of the wild daffodils . . .

DIRK BOGARDE
*A Short Walk from Harrods*

The valley of the Rhône is indescribable. I have never yet known what sunlight is; I have never seen autumn colours on trees. All along the Rhône there are multitudes of poplars. You know what we call 'old gold'; well, imagine that with the brightest possible sun gleaming upon it and you yet cannot conceive what these trees are like. And the vineyards, two hundred miles of them. The dead vine leaves are sometimes patches of brilliant scarlet. But how am I to describe the sunlight – the atmosphere, the distances?

GEORGE GISSING
in a letter to his sister Ellen, 28 October 1888

. . . a marvellous Châteauneuf-du-Pape which filled the mind, like a good breeze filling a sail, with the sunshine it had soaked up and the intensity of the hot soil of the Rhône valley . . . It brought to the brain a marvellous lucidity.

MARCEL ROUFF
*La Vie et la passion de Dodin-Bouffant*

Will any linguist tell me why Rhône is masculine, and Saône feminine? and whether there is any rule of philological philosophy or only more caprice in French genders?

MARTIN F. TUPPER
*Paterfamilias' Diary of Everybody's Tour*, 1856

A little on the other side of Lyons, our postilion exclaimed, 'Monte Bianco' and turning round, I beheld, for the first time, Mont Blanc, which had been hidden from us, when near it, by a fog. It looked like a turret in the sky, amber-coloured, golden.

LEIGH HUNT
*Autobiography*

All the affection I have for the French is for the whole nation, and it seems to be a little honey spread over all the bread I eat in their land.

MARY WOLLSTONECRAFT
in a letter to Ruth Barlow, February 1793

The Hôtel de la Poste hadn't altogether modernized its interior, but it contained much solid comfort and supplied the richest meals in Rouen. Consequently it was frequented by every British officer employed in the district.

SIEGFRIED SASSOON
*Memoirs of an Infantry Officer*

Whoever seems a little more distinguished than another has been to France.

GEORGE MOORE
*Confessions of a Young Man*, 1888

Morgan said there was often a good and friendly feeling between English and French soldiers when they were in the field. He had often been on picquet duty less than 50 yards from the French sentries. He would call out, 'Bon Soir'. The Frenchmen would sing out in return 'Will you boire?' Then they would lay down their arms, meet in the middle space and drink together. Morgan liked drinking with the French sentries because they mostly had something hot.

REVD FRANCIS KILVERT
*Diary*, 15 August 1870

Let the French but have England, and they won't want to conquer it.

HORACE WALPOLE
in a letter to the Hon H.S. Conway, 1 July 1745

Speaking as a true Norman, I have to say that while I bear a grudge against the Germans, I do not hate and resent them in the way that I hate the English – because they have invaded and plundered this land twenty times over, and because I inherited aversion for this perfidious nation from my forebears.

GUY DE MAUPASSANT
*Le Rosier de Madame Husson, 1888*

What strange prejudices we are apt to take regarding foreigners!

DR EDWARD RIGBY
*Letters from France in 1789*

I went early in the morning to obtain a *permis de séjour* (residential permit) at the police station. The secretary of the commissaire, the typical *chien de commissaire*, as Parisian slang has it, was rough and gruff as usual, so I was surprised when he suddenly said to me: 'Your soldiers have done splendid work in the north.' 'They have done their best,' I replied. 'Done their best,' he echoed, 'they've saved France!' This brought a lump into my throat. Only an Englishman who has lived for many years in Paris can appreciate what a tremendous thing this was for a Frenchman to say.

ROWLAND STRONG
*The Diary of an English Resident in France*, 1915

*Entente cordiale*: dead or alive? In reasonably good health, I think, but if its survival were left to the French it would be dead as a dodo.

Francophile RICHARD BINNS,
writing in *The Times*, October 1994

We are part of the continent of Europe, not just a balcony overlooking the Atlantic.
> FRANÇOIS MITTERRAND
> in *Libération*, November 1988

Not enough people in either country have grasped the essential fact: that in our interests, in our assets, in our view of Europe, in our hopes and fears for the outside world, there are no two substantial countries so similar as France and Britain.
> DOUGLAS HURD
> in a speech to the Franco-British Council,
> October 1994

England and France will always be sisters.
> VICTOR HUGO
> *Cromwell*